DAYS OF DECISION

Hitler and Kristallnacht

Edited by Andrew Farrow, Adrian Vigliano, and Mark Friedman
Designed by Cynthia Della-Rovere
Original illustrations © Capstone Global Library Ltd
Illustrated by H L Studios and Cynthia Della-Rovere
Picture research by Elizabeth Alexander
Production by Sophia Argyris
Originated by Capstone Global Library Ltd
Printed in China

ISBN 978 1 406 26150 9 (hardback)
17 16 15 14 13
10 9 8 7 6 5 4 3 2 1

ISBN 978 1 406 26157 8 (paperback)
17 16 15 14 13
10 9 8 7 6 5 4 3 2 1

British Library Cataloguing in Publication Data
A full catalogue record for this book is available from the British Library.

Acknowledgements
We would like to thank the following for permission to reproduce photographs: ©Corbis pp. 14, 42; ©Photoshot pp. 4, 13; Alamy p. 15t (©Pictorial Press Ltd); Corbis pp. 9, 19, 37, 39 (©Hulton-Deutsch Collection), 8 (Three Lions/Hulton Archive), 24, 35, 47, imprint page (©Bettmann), 52 (©Jacek Bednarczyk/epa); Gamma-Keystone via Getty Images pp. 17, 23 (Keystone-France); Getty Images pp. 11r (Hulton Archive), 10 (Galerie Bilderwelt), 18, 43 (Popperfoto), 20, 28, 33, 50 (Keystone/Hulton Archive), 31 (Central Press/Picture Post), 40 (Roger Viollet), 45 (Zoltan Kluger/GPO), 49 (Sean Gallup); Photoshot pp. 25 (© TALKING SPORT), 30 (© UPPA).

Background and design features reproduced with the permission of Shutterstock (©Picsfive, ©Petrov Stanislav, ©Zastolskiy Victor, ©design36, ©a454, ©Andreas Gradin, ©Potapov Alexander, ©Olemac).

Cover photograph of a portrait of Adolf Hitler reproduced with the permission of Superstock (ClassicStock.com); Cover photograph of the burning Synagogue of Hannover reproduced with the permission of Historisches Museum Hannover, HAZ-Hauschild-Archiv.

We would like to thank Dr Gerhard Wolf for his invaluable help in the preparation of this book.

Every effort has been made to contact copyright holders of any material reproduced in this book. Any omissions will be rectified in subsequent printings if notice is given to the publisher.

Contents

Some words are printed in **bold**, like this. You can find out what they mean by looking in the glossary on page 59.

A night of broken glass

On the night of 9 November 1938, violence ripped through communities across Germany and Austria. The violence was aimed solely at Jews. Crowds of **civilians** and **Nazi** Party members set fire to **synagogues**, beat up Jewish people, and destroyed and **looted** Jews' stores and homes. Smashed glass from shop windows glittered like crystals on the streets, and the horrific episode became known as Kristallnacht, or "Crystal Night".

Throughout Germany and Austria, Nazi thugs destroyed hundreds of Jewish synagogues, burning or stealing the sacred objects inside.

Declaring war on Jews

The violence continued throughout the next day. At least 90 Jewish people died, and 30,000 Jewish men were arrested and sent to prison camps.[1] Countless others were injured, humiliated, or driven from their homes. The savagery of the attacks sent shock waves around the globe. The *Times* newspaper condemned "the tale of burnings and beatings, of blackguardly [brutal] assaults on defenceless and innocent people, which disgraced [Germany] yesterday".[2]

Today, we view this "night of broken glass" as a murderous turning point in 20th-century history. Five years earlier, in 1933, Adolf Hitler and his Nazi Party had come to power and immediately begun their campaign against Jews. Hitler had forced through a series of laws that deprived German Jews of their rights. The Nazis started a systematic campaign to encourage them to leave the country.

Then came the decision to attack Jewish people, their homes, and their property on Kristallnacht. With this, Hitler took his **persecution** of German Jews a step further. It was a decisive turn in anti-Jewish policies, and it announced to the whole world that a terrible threat faced the Jews of Europe.

What does Nazi mean?

The word "Nazi" is short for *nationalsozialistisch*, which is German for "National Socialist". It came from the name of the German political party led by Hitler, *Nationalsozialistische Deutsche Arbeiterpartei*, or NSDAP. The Nazi Party was founded under another name in 1919. Hitler became its leader in 1921, and governed Germany from 1933 to 1945. The Nazi use of the term "socialist" is just one meaning of several. Socialist usually refers to the **communist** system of government, in which the state owns the means of producing and distributing goods, and in which people are treated equally. But the Nazi Party was very different. It promoted "national" socialism, in which rights were reserved for ethnic Germans, and it was fiercely anti-communist.

Hitler's horrific intentions

The events of Kristallnacht were no accident – they were deliberately planned. Although many civilians took part, members of the Nazi Party led and organized the riots. Officials directed bands of Nazis to attack Jewish property and people. They wore civilian clothes and carried sledgehammers and other tools. The police were ordered not to stop them. The fire departments were told only to put out fires that threatened non-Jewish property.

Behind it all was one man: Adolf Hitler. He did not make the plans or give direct orders, but the officials knew what he wanted. For many years, Hitler had argued that Germany must get rid of every single Jew, as part of his programme of "purifying" the country's population. He and other Nazis believed that true Germans (whom he called "**Aryans**") were a superior race, and that Jewish people were inferior. The Nazis believed Jews must be forced to **emigrate** – and later that they should be killed.

The Jews of Europe

The Jewish people are descended from the Hebrews, who lived in the Middle East thousands of years ago. Eventually Jews settled in what is now Israel. They also developed Judaism, one of the oldest major faiths in the world.

Their land was conquered many times, and most Jews were driven out, gradually spreading throughout Europe, Asia, and Africa. This **emigration** is called the Diaspora, meaning "exile", or being forced to live abroad. By 1200, there were thriving Jewish communities in many parts of the world, including Spain, Poland, Russia, India, and the Islamic Empire of the Middle East.

This map shows the distribution of Jewish people throughout Europe during the 1930s.

The beginning of anti-Semitism

Jews were always a minority group wherever they settled. Even in the early Middle Ages they were seen as outsiders, and Christians and other non-Jews **persecuted** them in many different ways. This **discrimination** against the Jewish people is called **anti-Semitism**.

Over the centuries, many false rumours grew about the Jews, which led to acts of hatred and violence against them. These delusions made people unfairly accuse the Jewish people of:

- *Performing blood sacrifice*: Many Jews lived in majority Christian countries. Christians condemned them as the race that had killed Jesus, the founder of the Christian faith. A rumour grew that Jews murdered Christian children and drank their blood.[1]

- *Well poisoning*: In medieval times, many people accused Jews of poisoning wells and spreading disease. Jews were blamed for the disastrous epidemic of plague called the Black Death in 1347. Similar accusations have been made in modern times.[2]

- *Planning to take over the world*: Many people believed that a group of powerful rabbis (Jewish spiritual leaders) was plotting to take over the world.

- *Being obsessed with money*: In many countries, Jews could not own land or belong to guilds (craft organizations). One of the few occupations they were allowed was money lending, a trade that Christians despised – though it was essential. This inspired the unjust image of the miserly Jewish moneylender.

Pogroms and emancipation

For many centuries, the Jews of Europe suffered from the hatred of their neighbours. In 1096, fanatical Christians murdered at least 10,000 Jews in France and Germany.[3] In 1506, hundreds of Jews were slaughtered in Lisbon, Portugal, because they were blamed for a famine. In the early 1650s, at least 100,000 Jews were killed during uprisings in Ukraine.[4] **Massacres** such as these were known as **pogroms**.

However, starting in the late 18th century, many European countries began to pass laws that gave Jews better protection and rights, such as worshipping freely and owning property. In 1791, France was the first country to do this. Other countries followed, including Britain in 1858, and Germany in 1871.

The disaster of World War I

By 1914, most European Jews had legal rights. But they still faced persecution from **anti-Semites** in many countries. In Germany there was a strong **nationalist** movement, which included many who believed that the German *volk* (people) should be a racially pure people, unspoiled by foreign blood. Jews, even though they had lived in Germany for centuries, were seen as foreigners.

There were severe shortages in Germany following World War I. Some people were forced to search for food amid the rubbish in the streets.

Jews in the German army

In 1914, there were an estimated 555,000 native Jews in Germany. More than 100,000 of these fought for their country during World War I. At least 12,000 were killed in battle.[6]

This **racist** feeling was made more bitter by the events of World War I (1914–1918). German aggression against its neighbours in 1914 contributed to the start of the war, which ended in humiliating defeat and economic ruin for Germany, with more than 1.7 million of its soldiers dead. Ashamed and angry about the disaster, many Germans looked for a scapegoat (someone they could blame). They quickly found one: the Jewish population.

Many new false rumours developed. Some people said that Jews had avoided the front-line fighting and had grown rich from the profits of the war. Some people even believed Germany had only lost the war because the Jews had betrayed the country to its enemies.[5]

The young Adolf Hitler

Adolf Hitler was one of the many soldiers who fought for Germany in World War I. Born in Austria in 1889, he was brought up by a doting mother and a harsh father. After unsuccessful periods as a student and a painter, he moved to Munich, Germany, in 1913.

Hitler joined the German army in 1914. He served as a messenger in the war, often in the front line, and was awarded the Iron Cross medal for courageous actions. He was thrilled by army life, which gave him a sense of belonging. He called this "the greatest and most unforgettable time of my earthly existence".[7]

Germany's defeat in 1918 was a massive shock to Hitler. Like many others, he was convinced that Jewish traitors were responsible for Germany's defeat. He already had strong anti-Semitic views, but these now began turning to ferocious racial hatred. Jews, he believed, were part of an inferior race that was separate from the Germans. He concluded that they had to be removed.

Adolf Hitler (right) served as a dispatch runner during World War I. He believed passionately that Germany was right to go to war.

Decisive words: the Gemlich letter

"Everything men strive after as a higher goal, be it religion, socialism, democracy, is to the Jew only means to an end, the way to satisfy his lust for gold and domination. In his effects he is like a racial tuberculosis [deadly disease] of the nations.

Anti-Semitism … must lead to the systematic elimination of the privileges of the Jews… The ultimate objective must be the irrevocable [not capable of being undone] removal of the Jews in general."[8]

Adolf Hitler, in a letter to a fellow soldier, Adolf Gemlich, 16 September 1919

9

Hitler's rise to power

In September 1919, Hitler joined a small political group called the German Workers' Party. He soon became its leading figure. The party changed its name to the National Socialist German Worker's Party. From then on, it was known as the Nazi Party.

Party leader

In February 1920, the Nazis published a list of their aims. At the top was the creation of a larger "German Nation", which would include territory lost after World War I. But another demand was included: "None but members of the Nation may be citizens of the State. None but those of German blood may be members of the Nation. No Jew, therefore, may be a member of the Nation."[1]

Hitler had helped to draft the anti-Jewish parts of the programme. By now, he was growing more passionate about what he saw as the Jewish threat to Germany. He even thought up a new slogan: "Anti-Semites of the World, Unite!"[2] But the Nazis were not alone. There were many **extremist** groups in Germany that had the same racist ideas.

Nazi storm troopers of the SA in their brown shirts marched through the streets of Munich. They were ordered to disrupt the meetings of rival politicians, and to protect Hitler from attacks by his enemies.

In July 1921, Hitler took control of the Nazi Party and made it a more military and violent organization. He formed a uniformed group of thugs to control meetings and frighten or beat up his opponents. This was called the *Sturmabteilung* ("Storm Section", or **SA**), and its members were known as **storm troopers**. The party took as its emblem the ancient symbol of the swastika.

Putsch and prison

Hitler's hatred of the Jews was mixed up with hatred of the **Bolsheviks** (Russian communists). Since they had seized power in Russia after the Russian Revolution (see the box on the right), the Bolsheviks' ideals had swept across Europe. Like many Germans, Hitler believed the Bolsheviks wanted to dominate the world. This put them in league with the Jews, who were also accused of plotting a global takeover.

Germany was a deeply divided nation at this time, with a struggling post-war economy. Many rival parties were fighting for power. Hitler was worried that the communists would take power in his local region of Bavaria, and so he decided to strike first. On 8 November 1923, he led a **putsch** (revolt) aimed at seizing control of the Bavarian government. It failed, and Hitler and other Nazis were sent to prison for treason (attempting to overthrow their government).

The Russian Revolution

In 1917, a series of uprisings in Russia overthrew the tsar (emperor). By October, the Bolsheviks ruled the country and began the process of transforming it into a communist state. It became the **Soviet Union** (USSR) in the 1920s.

Prison writing

While he was imprisoned, Hitler began writing a book called *Mein Kampf*, meaning "My Struggle". At its centre was the belief that Germans were a superior race and should control the world. Hitler outlined in great detail his reasons for hating the Jewish people.

Hitler had an easy life in Landsberg Prison, where he was sent after his trial in 1923. He had a large, comfortable room and was treated with great respect by his guards.

The Nazis lose ground

Thanks to powerful supporters, Hitler served less than one year of a five-year prison sentence. But because of the putsch, the Nazi Party had been greatly weakened. Hitler was banned from speaking in public in most of Germany until 1927.[3] Partly because the economy was strong, the Nazis gained little support at this time. In the 1928 election, they had just 2.6 per cent of the vote.[4]

The German economy was recovering, thanks to massive loans from the United States. Industry and employment grew, and moderate politicians ran the government. In this atmosphere, many people turned away from extremist parties like the Nazis.

But Hitler was convinced his political ideas were correct and that he would eventually be Germany's leader. The first step was to re-launch the Nazi Party in February 1925 and make it better known. The second was to take total control of the party. He told members: "I alone lead the movement, and no one can impose conditions on me. I bear the whole responsibility for everything that occurs in the movement."[5]

Hitler reorganized the Nazis and gained new members. Over the next four years, numbers rose from 27,000 to 178,000.[6] Hitler appointed men to head important units inside the party. These included Joseph Goebbels, who took charge of **propaganda**.

Joseph Goebbels 1897–1945

Born: Rheydt, in the Ruhr district of Germany

Role: Nazi politician and minister of propaganda

As a young man, Joseph Goebbels was an unsuccessful writer, and he failed to get into the army because he was very short and had a lame leg. This made him bitter. He joined the Nazi Party, and in 1926 he became a devoted follower of Hitler. "Hitler is great," he said. "I bow to the greater one, the political genius."[7] Goebbels established the Nazis in Berlin and was elected to the **Reichstag** (German parliament) in 1928. He was made minister of propaganda in 1933 and showed brilliant skill at controlling mass opinion.

Did you know? As a young man, Goebbels wanted to be a great writer. But all his plays and novels were rejected. Goebbels was convinced that all publishers were Jewish and were refusing work by Aryans.

Starting in 1927, the Nazis held an annual rally at Nuremberg, in central Germany. The main aim of the rallies was to glorify and strengthen the reputation of their leader, Adolf Hitler.

Economic crisis

Germany was plunged into crisis once more in 1929. An economic **depression** spread across the world following a financial crash in the United States. Germany was especially badly hit by this depression. Businesses failed, unemployment soared (eventually reaching over 6 million in 1932), welfare systems collapsed, and there were shortages of food and other essential supplies.[8]

The chaos and misery of the period of depression made people angry with their democratic government. Support for extremist groups like the Nazis increased. People looked for strong leaders, and Hitler's promises of violent change gave them hope. Germans also looked again for someone to blame. Hitler's increasing hatred of the Jews, whom he saw as both greedy financiers and threatening Bolsheviks, gave them an easy target.

What do you think?

Did the economic depression aid Hitler?

Would Hitler have grown so powerful if the world's economies had never entered a depression? Without the misery and poverty caused by the economic depression, the Nazis might have remained a small minority party. See what you can find out about this period. Get started by looking at www.historyplace.com/worldwar2/riseofhitler/begins.htm.

Powerful backers

The misery and desperation of the economic depression gave Hitler the chance to gain real popularity. In the general election of September 14 1930, the Nazi Party won 107 seats, making it the second-largest party in the Reichstag.[9] Now people began to realize how much influence Hitler had in Germany. Among them were two very powerful sections of the population: the army and the wealthy **industrialists**.

Parades by the massed ranks of the SS formed a major part of the Nuremberg rallies. They carried swastika standards with the motto "*Deutschland Erwache*" ("Germany, Awake").

Hitler the orator

Much of Hitler's success was due to his dramatic speeches, which moved and excited huge crowds wherever he spoke. He would begin quietly and hesitantly and gradually increase in volume and speed. Using his hands to emphasize points, he would grow more passionate, barking out short sentences, mocking his enemies, and hammering home his arguments. Like an actor, he rehearsed his performances carefully.

Since Germany's defeat in World War I, Germany's once powerful army had been limited to just 100,000 men. Many officers were ashamed about this, and they felt that Hitler offered a chance to restore the armed forces. Leaders of German industry and finance also saw that the Nazis would resist Germany's strong Social Democratic and Communist parties, and introduce policies to help make banks and industry wealthier. They decided to support Hitler, and gave large donations of money.

Winning over Germany

The extra money helped the Nazis to pay for better organization and publicity in election campaigns. This, together with Hitler's rousing speeches, brought another huge boost in the party's popularity. In the election of 31 July 1932, the Nazis took 230 seats and became the biggest party in the Reichstag.[10] But it was not enough to take power, and an alliance of more moderate parties ruled Germany.

At this stage, Hitler was trying to disguise the brutality of his policies. Instead of preaching simple hatred for the Jewish people, he promoted racial purity. He said that an Aryan people, cleaned of all "alien" elements, could build a glorious future and rule the world. He hoped this would reassure people and make them vote for him. Another election was held in November 1932, but no party gained enough seats to govern.

This Nazi Party poster for the 1932 German elections shows a heroic farmer figure getting rid of the usual Nazi targets: Jewish financiers, Communists, and journalists.

Hitler tried to create an atmosphere of alarm. He claimed the communists were planning a revolution. Meanwhile, **SS** squads (see the box below) increased violent attacks on communists and Jews. Industrial leaders, worried by the chaos, increased their backing of Hitler. At last, on 30 January 1933, the German president, Paul von Hindenburg, appointed Hitler as the country's new **chancellor**. This gave him real power at last. The president was important, but the chancellor was in charge of the real daily business of government.

Himmler and the SS

In 1925, Hitler formed a small new unit called the *Schutzstaffel* ("Protection Squadron"), also known as the SS. This was separate from the SA (storm troopers) and provided bodyguards for Nazi leaders. In 1929, Hitler appointed Heinrich Himmler as SS leader. Born in 1900, Himmler had joined the Nazi Party in 1923. Under him, the SS developed into a security force with enormous power, including the power of identifying people's ethnic background. They wore black uniforms and their caps had skull and crossbones badges. The SS later took charge of running **concentration camps** and **death camps**.

The persecution begins

The Nazis were not the only party that wanted to get rid of Germany's Jews. During the 1920s, many nationalist groups had called for the racial "cleansing" of the population and encouraged violence against Jewish Germans. But after Hitler was appointed chancellor in 1933, anti-Semitism actually became the official policy of the German government.

Hitler, the Führer

To make sure he kept his power, Hitler tried to destroy all his rivals. He was now addressed as the **Führer** (leader). He declared that the only way to make Germany great again was by ruthlessly following the Nazi programme and tolerating no opposition. "Those unwilling to be converted must be crushed," he told senior army leaders.[1] His aim was to make his power absolute and unchallenged.

Hitler began by destroying the Communist Party and other left-wing (liberal) groups. He made their meetings illegal, and storm troopers attacked trade union members and communists. On 27 February 1933, the Reichstag in Berlin was burned down. Nazi leaders believed this was the start of a revolution and ordered mass arrests. At least 25,000 communists were imprisoned in the province of Prussia alone.[2]

The Nazis went on to seize control of all

Making Germany great again

Hitler came to power with a programme of measures that aimed to restore Germany's place in the world as a powerful nation. Two of these measures have been described here – smashing the communist threat and "purifying" the German race. But the Nazis had two other big aims:

- Expanding German territory: Hitler believed the German population needed more *lebensraum* ("living space") so that they could grow powerful. This meant expanding eastwards, into Eastern European countries and Russia.

- Reversing the Treaty of Versailles: After World War I, Germany had been forced to sign the Treaty of Versailles, which imposed many conditions, including the loss of territory and a limit to the size of the armed forces. Hitler was determined to break these conditions, reclaiming lost lands and expanding the German military.

areas of power. They occupied town halls, trade union centres, and newspaper offices, and took over commercial and local government organizations. Local German police forces were brought together under Nazi rule, including the **Gestapo**, which was the secret police.

Violence against the Jews

At the same time, there were attacks on Jews across the land. Starting in early March, these attacks spread from the Ruhr (a major industrial region) to Berlin, Hamburg, and the southwest.[3]

Gangs of storm troopers roamed the streets, beating up Jews and anyone who they thought looked Jewish. Jewish-owned shops

The Nazis banned relationships between Aryans and Jewish people. This German woman and Jewish man are being forced to wear signs to embarrass them.

were looted, and Jewish lawyers and judges were barred from practising. A number of Jews died in this first wave of mayhem.

How did anti-Semitic violence fit in with Hitler's aims? Nazis had previously condemned Jewish people as supporters of the Bolsheviks. But if the Communist Party was smashed, how could the Jews be seen as a threat? Hitler solved this question by portraying them as a danger to the racial purity of Germany.

The first concentration camp

The Nazis arrested huge numbers of people suspected of being critics or enemies of the new government. Starting in early March 1933, many of the detainees were sent to a prison camp at Dachau, near the city of Munich. The prison camp was converted from an old factory and could hold 5,000 prisoners.[4] Dachau grew into the first of the Nazi concentration camps.

Dachau was a brutal place, established to punish people by working them to death. When the camp opened, the SS commander told his men: "You all know what the Führer [Hitler] has called upon us to do. We haven't come here to treat those swine inside like human beings. Any man who can't stand the sight of blood doesn't belong here. The more of these [prisoners] we shoot, the fewer we'll have to feed."[5]

Political opponents of the Nazis were held in the first concentration camp at Dachau.

Many people in other countries were shocked at the atrocities in Germany. Yet foreign governments were slow to express their horror and took no practical action against Hitler.

Jewish groups and other campaign groups tried to bring the growing disaster to the world's attention. In the United States and Europe, there were **boycotts** of German goods. For a time, the campaign threatened to damage Germany's important trading links with the outside world.

Exclusion of the Jews

Hitler blamed these demonstrations on the Jewish people. He ordered a full-scale boycott of Jewish businesses and goods throughout Germany. This took place on 1 April 1933. SA storm troopers stopped people from entering Jewish shops and plastered doors and windows with notices saying "Jews Out!" and "Perish Judah!"[6]

Then, on 7 April, the Nazis passed a new law dismissing from the civil service (government jobs) anyone who was "not of Aryan descent" and who was seen as politically unreliable.[7] In practice, this meant that all Jewish civil servants were sacked. For the first time, the population had been legally divided into two parts: Germans and Jews.

At the start of the boycott of Jewish businesses in 1933, storm troopers put up warning posters on shop windows. This one said "Germans! Defend yourselves! Do not buy from Jews!"

Other targets

Jews formed by far the largest group targeted by the Nazis. But other minorities also suffered severe persecution and were eventually sent to death camps. These included the mentally ill, homosexuals, the **Roma** (also called Gypsies, though this is a term Roma do not like), and the Jehovah's Witnesses, a Christian sect whose members refused to join the Nazi Party or serve in the military.

Jews were often attacked or humiliated in public in Germany. But few ordinary Germans took part in the persecution during this period. People experienced a huge amount of anti-Jewish propaganda broadcast by Goebbels and other government departments, and many people probably believed it. Even so, most were at first horrified by the violence and hatred on display. Many were also afraid to speak out because of possible punishments from the Nazis. In the years to come, these attitudes would change.

How did the Jewish community react?

When Hitler came to power, there were more than 500,000 Jews living in Germany. Most had been born there and were a permanent part of German society. They had suffered some persecution during the 1920s, but the anti-Semitic campaigns of early 1933 were on a much bigger scale. During that year, about 37,000 Jews left Germany to settle in friendlier countries.[8]

However, many Jews decided to stay in Germany. They believed the Nazis would not remain in power for long and that the anti-Jewish laws would eventually be abolished. Jewish communities also united and began developing ways to overcome their problems. When Jews were excluded from many areas of German society, they formed organizations to provide Jewish schools and welfare services and help Jewish artists and athletes.[9]

Deceit and cunning

Though anti-Semitic violence continued from 1933 into 1934, there was a lull in government action against the Jews. Hitler knew that **sanctions** by other countries would harm Germany's economic recovery. He was anxious to make a good impression

Hermann Goering was a long-term Nazi Party member, and one of Hitler's most trusted colleagues. Greedy and flamboyant, he used his position to make himself very wealthy.

and convince foreign leaders that his plans were peaceful. "We respect the national rights of other people," he declared, "and wish to live with them in peace and friendship."[10]

At the same time, Hitler wanted to build up his armed forces. Nazi leaders, including Hermann Goering, planned to increase it from the 100,000 men allowed in the Treaty of Versailles (see page 16) to at least 300,000. But they needed permission from the League of Nations. When this was refused in October 1933, Hitler took Germany out of the League of Nations.

League of Nations

The League of Nations was an international organization set up in 1919, after World War I. Its aim was to preserve peace and settle arguments through debates and council decisions. Many countries were members (though not the United States), but the league never had any real power. After Germany and Japan withdrew in 1933, it became even weaker. After World War II (1939–1945), it was replaced by the United Nations.

Soon, Hitler's plans for military expansion went ahead. In January 1934, he made a pact (agreement) with neighbouring Poland, pledging that neither country would attack the other. This gave Germany an ally (friendly country) on its eastern border. In March 1935, the Nazis announced a new system of military service. All German men within a certain age group would be called up for training. This measure was aimed at doubling the size of the forces in a single year.

Hermann Goering 1893–1946

Born: Bavaria

Role: Nazi minister and commander of the Luftwaffe (German Air Force)

Hermann Goering was a famous fighter pilot in World War I. He joined the Nazi Party in 1922, was elected to the Reichstag in 1928, and became one of Hitler's most powerful supporters. In 1933, he founded the Nazi Gestapo, the secret police force. He used the Gestapo to help crush the growing power of the SA in 1934 (see page 22). He also began to build up the Luftwaffe, which broke the conditions of the Treaty of Versailles.

Did you know? Goering made a huge fortune during the Nazi period from seizing Jewish belongings and wealth. He took property himself and also took bribes for allowing others to do so.

Total power

Two events in 1934 raised Hitler to the position of a **dictator** with absolute control of Germany. The first took place between 30 June and 2 July. Hitler was alarmed by the growing power and size of the SA, which threatened to run out of control and take over the German army, so he took decisive steps. SS units were ordered to seize and murder the SA leaders. At least 85 men died in what Hitler later called "the Night of the Long Knives."[11]

Fascism in Europe: Mussolini and Franco

Hitler was not the only right-wing dictator in Europe during the 1930s. In Italy, Benito Mussolini had developed **fascism** in the 1920s. Fascism, like Nazism, was based on nationalism, obedience to the leader, and military might. Hitler and Mussolini became allies in 1936. There were also fascist leaders in several other European countries, including Spain, where Francisco Franco ruled as dictator until his death in 1975.

The episode made Hitler even more popular among Germans, many of whom saw it as strong action to stop a dangerous rebellion. This wave of approval made his next move easier. On 2 August, the German president, Paul von Hindenburg, died. Hitler immediately made himself president, so that he was both head of state and chancellor. He now had no rivals – and total power.

The Nuremberg Laws

At the start of 1935, Hitler was in a stronger position than ever. He was dictator of Germany, and after leaving the League of Nations, he knew that he could defy the rest of Europe. Even so, he continued to act cautiously about his policy towards the Jews, and he stressed that Germany only wanted to live peacefully with other nations. He hoped this would calm international anger over Nazi plans for violating the Treaty of Versailles by calling up many men to join the military.

But behind the scenes, new anti-Jewish measures were being drawn up. Hitler announced them at the Nazi Party Rally at Nuremberg on 15 September 1935. The two new laws – known as the Nuremberg Laws – officially separated Jewish people from the German state. They were:

After Hitler came to power, the Nuremberg Rallies had grown into massive and well-drilled displays of power, involving as many as 700,000 people.

- *The Citizenship Law:* According to the Citizenship Law, only people with four German grandparents were considered German citizens. Anyone with at least one Jewish grandparent was classed as Jewish. It was not for the individual to decide whether he or she was Jewish. This law classified as Jews people who did not necessarily see themselves as Jews, or who were in fact Christians because they or their parents had already converted.

- *The Blood Law:* According to the Blood Law, marriage between Jews and German citizens was forbidden. Sexual relations outside marriage between Jews and Germans were forbidden. Jews could not raise or display the German flag.

Although trying to hide his true feelings of hatred – in order to deceive foreign leaders – Hitler had probably ordered the preparation of these laws. But other Nazi leaders, such as Interior Minister Wilhelm Frick, actually prepared the laws. Hitler decided to announce the laws at the Nuremberg Rally, in order to make a dramatic impression.

Decisive words: dehumanizing the Jewish people

"The Jew is the creation of a different God. If I put the Aryan next to the Jew and call the former a man, then I have to call the other by another name. They are as far apart as the animal is from the human. Not that I want to call the Jew an animal. He is a being foreign to nature and removed from nature."[12]

Adolf Hitler, in conversation with German politician Hermann Rauschning, 1934

23

The Nazi grip tightens

With the Nuremberg Laws, Hitler had showed the world his true attitude towards the Jews in Germany. These laws defined Jews officially as outsiders who were racially separated from other Germans. But this was just the beginning. Over the next three years, the Nazi treatment of Jews became even more brutal. At the same time, Hitler took bolder steps to rearm and to expand Germany's territory – in defiance of world opinion.

Forced emigration

What was Hitler's ultimate plan for the Jews? In his speeches and conversations, he expressed hatred and disgust for the Jewish race and vowed to remove Jews from German society. But at this stage, he had no definite method for achieving this. The idea of a "Final Solution" involving the **genocide** of European Jews would not become Nazi policy until 1941 (see page 41).

It is likely Hitler believed that increasing state persecution would simply drive Jews out of the country. In 1937, Goebbels recorded Hitler's views in his diary, writing: "The Jew must get out of Germany, yes out of the whole of Europe. That will take some time. But it will and must happen. The Führer is firmly decided on it."[1]

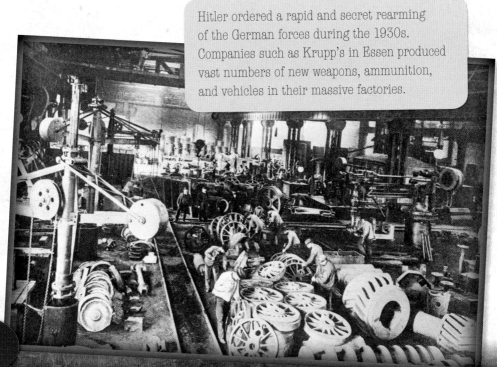

Hitler ordered a rapid and secret rearming of the German forces during the 1930s. Companies such as Krupp's in Essen produced vast numbers of new weapons, ammunition, and vehicles in their massive factories.

Taking a gamble

Germany had been secretly rebuilding its armed forces since 1933. By 1936, it had an army of 300,000 men and a large fleet of fighter planes. Now the production of new weapons, ships, and planes gathered speed, as the military took over more German factories and shipyards. In fact, the **rearmament** programme not only created a powerful armed force, but it also helped create employment and wealth for industrialists.

What do you think?

Why did Britain and France fail to act?

Why did Britain and France fail to take action when Hitler started rebuilding German armed forces? He was clearly breaking the Treaty of Versailles. Were they frightened of him? Or did they think he posed no threat? Find out more about this on sites such as:

www.historylearningsite.co.uk/germany_and_rearmament.htm

Although the Nazis were breaking the terms of the Treaty of Versailles, few European governments protested strongly. This lack of opposition made Hitler bolder, and he ordered an even more aggressive act. Since 1919, Germany had been forbidden from stationing troops in the Rhineland region. On 7 March 1936, German soldiers marched into the region, where they were greeted with flowers and cheers. There was no opposition from the French or British.

The Berlin Olympics

On 1 August 1936, the Olympic Games opened in Berlin, and visitors from all over the world flocked to Germany. Hitler saw it as a chance to enhance Nazi prestige, and he spent huge amounts of money on impressing foreigners with lavish presentations and grand spectacles.

Hitler believed that black people were inferior to Aryans. But he was embarrassed at the 1936 Olympics, when the American athlete Jesse Owens won four gold medals, defeating his German rivals.

Attempts to expel the Jews

Once the Olympics were over, the Nazi government began to make life even harder for German Jews. Goering and Reinhard Heydrich set up a department for enforcing new currency laws against Jews. These laws were so strict that most Jews were forced to pay heavy fines or simply have their wealth taken away from them. This had a double benefit for the Nazis – they not only stole Jewish money, but they also used it to pay for rearmament.[2]

The economic pressure grew worse. On 1 December 1936, a new law threatened the death penalty to anyone who moved his or her money abroad. This was clearly aimed at Jews. Meanwhile, the boycott of Jewish stores and other suppliers went on. Soon most Jews were finding it difficult to earn any money at all. Many were forced to sell their businesses cheaply to non-Jews.

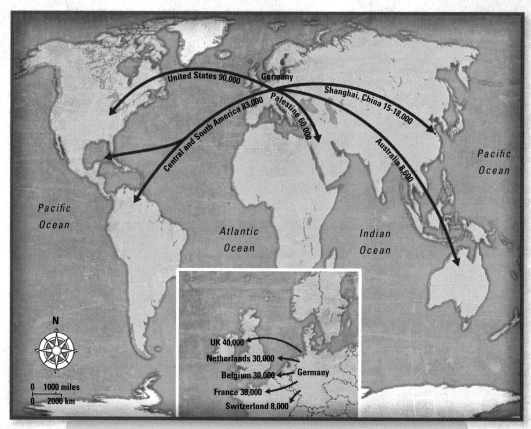

This map shows the main destinations of Jewish people emigrating from Germany in the 1930s. The numbers are complicated by the fact that often the same person fled twice: for example, first to France and then to Britain, and maybe later on to the United States or Palestine.

Where did the Jews go?

The clear purpose of Hitler and his ministers was to drive the Jewish people out of Germany. A government paper published in 1937 stated that Nazi policy regarding Jews was entirely focused on "convincing the Jewish population that its only way out is emigration".[3] But where could Jewish people leaving Germany go? Many moved to neighbouring European countries such as France, Belgium, Poland, and Switzerland. Others settled in various locations around the world, including in Britain, the United States, China, Australia, and parts of Central and South America.

One of the most prized destinations was Palestine – the area in the Middle East that now contains Israel. This was the place where the Jewish people had originally lived 2,000 years before. Starting in the 1890s, some had returned there, hoping to establish a Jewish homeland. Many thousands more moved to Palestine from Germany after the Nazis came to power in 1933.

Britain and Palestine

After centuries of Turkish rule, Palestine came under British control following World War I. But the new governors had a difficult task. In 1917, Arthur Balfour, the British foreign minister, had promised support for a Jewish homeland in the country. This meant the British had to cope with competing land claims from both Jewish settlers and native Arabs. At first, there was an uneasy peace between the two communities, but the mass settlement of German Jews led to Arab protests and violence from 1936 to 1939. During the long uprising, over 5,000 Arabs were killed by British soldiers.[5]

However, the arrival of such a large number of **refugees** angered the Palestinian **Arabs** who already lived in the country. They saw the incoming Jews as a threat to remove them from their homes. In April 1936, the Arabs began a series of attacks on the newcomers and their property, and the Jews fought back. By the end of 1937, at least 113 Jews had died in the conflict, as well as 15 Arabs.[4]

Seizing Austria

By the end of 1937, Germany's economy was much healthier – partly because of the huge amount of wealth the government was taking from the Jewish population. The country's armed forces were growing rapidly. Nazi troops had moved into the Rhineland, and no foreign action had been taken against them. Hitler knew that he was now in a strong position and could defy international opinion.

Hitler's next target was expansion into his homeland, Austria. In March 1938, he forced the resignation of the Austrian chancellor and replaced him with a Nazi called Arthur Seyss-Inquart. Seyss-Inquart declared that Austria was now united with Germany and invited German troops to occupy the country. This event was known as the Anschluss, or "Link-Up".

Vast crowds greeted Hitler during a victory parade through Vienna, Austria's capital, after the 1938 Anschluss.

A new wave of anti-Semitism

The majority of the population of Austria welcomed the Anschluss. But for the 180,000 Jews living there, it was a disaster.[6] They were immediately hit by all the measures that had already been imposed on German Jews – the Nuremberg Laws, the widespread boycott of their shops and businesses, and seizure of their property.

Austrian Jews had suffered racial violence before the Anschluss, but now it increased massively. Just as in Germany, SA storm troopers and SS men handed out beatings, insults, and humiliation to those who were not Aryan. The shock was so great that at least 500 Jews committed suicide within a month of the Nazi takeover.[7] In both Germany and Austria, Jews continued to be arrested and sent to prison camps, although there was no general wave of arrrests after the seizing of Austria. In the summer of 1938, the Nazis also began a new kind of anti-Semitic action by destroying and looting synagogues.

Who were the Aryans?

The Aryans were once thought to be a people who settled in northern India in prehistoric times. Many scholars now think this theory is mistaken, but little is known for certain.

Hitler, however, believed passionately that Germans were the descendants of the Aryans and were a master race, superior to all others. The typical Aryan, he thought, would have light skin, fair hair, and blue eyes, with a strong body and a noble mind. But historians have proved that Hitler was wrong. The Germans were not descended from the Aryans, but are a product of a great mixture of people, including the Romans who extended their empire to what was to become south and west Germany, and many Slavic people in the east.

Decisive words: settlement on Madagascar

"We're now proceeding more radically. The Führer wants gradually to push them [the Jews] all out. Negotiate with Poland and Romania. Madagascar would be the most suitable for them."[8]

Joseph Goebbels records Hitler's thoughts in his diary, 23 April 1938

Does this mark a change in Hitler's ideas for the future of the German Jews? Before, he wanted **emigrants** to be scattered around the world. Here, he suggests the entire Jewish community should be forcibly resettled on Madagascar, a French colony. This isolated island off southeast Africa was seen as a suitable place for abandoning unwanted people. However, the failure to defeat Britain, and the **Allies**' control of the seas, meant that the plan could not be carried out.

Decision time

The longer Hitler was in power, the more confident he became. It was clear that no one in Europe would oppose him directly, because they were anxious to avoid another catastrophic world war. Most European leaders believed Hitler was a reasonable man who wanted peace, so they agreed to his demands. This policy was known as appeasement.

This atmosphere gave Hitler the opportunity for his next bold step. The Sudetenland was a region on Germany's southeastern border that had been German territory until 1919. Now it was part of Czechoslovakia, but it had a large German population. In May 1938, Hitler announced that Germany would take over the Sudetenland. If any country opposed him, he threatened to invade all of Czechoslovakia.

UK and French leaders at first rejected the proposal. But in the end, desperate to keep peace, they gave in. On 29 September, at a meeting in Munich, they signed an agreement granting the Sudetenland to Germany. By 10 October, German forces were in control of the region.

The Nazi persecution even targeted Jewish students. The blackboard behind these Jewish boys displays the Star of David, a Jewish symbol. Underneath is written "The Jew is our greatest enemy. Beware of the Jew!"

Jewish emigration, 1933–1938

The following table shows the number of Jews leaving Germany for other countries:

Year	Number of Jews
1933	37,000 (out of a total Jewish population of 505,000[3])
1934	23,000
1935	21,000
1936	25,000
1937	23,000
1938	40,000[4]

Forced out

Meanwhile, the savage campaign to drive out Germany's Jews continued. But Nazi leaders were impatient, because it was not working quickly enough. By the autumn of 1938, only about one-third of over 800,000 people classed as Jews had emigrated, despite the persecution.[1]

The Nazis tried a new method of "racial cleansing". On 27 October, police began rounding up all the Jews who were Polish citizens. Many had lived in Germany since the end of World War I, or been born there, but now they were deported to Poland. Over 18,000 were forced over the border, but the Polish government refused entry to most of them.[2]

The Jews were stuck between two countries, crammed together in the bitter cold and damp, with little food or shelter. Some died or became ill in the appalling conditions. One girl managed to send a postcard to her brother in Paris, describing her ordeal. The brother's name was Herschel Grynszpan. On 6 November, he went to the German embassy in Paris to get revenge and shot a German official called Ernst vom Rath.

Foreign rejection of the Jews

A major obstacle to Jewish emigration was that many countries would only accept limited numbers. At an international conference at Evian, France, to discuss the crisis in July 1938, most countries (including Britain, the United States, Palestine, and Argentina) tightened up their rules for admitting emigrants. The delegate from Australia, T. W. White, said, "As we have no racial problem, we are not desirous of importing one."[5]

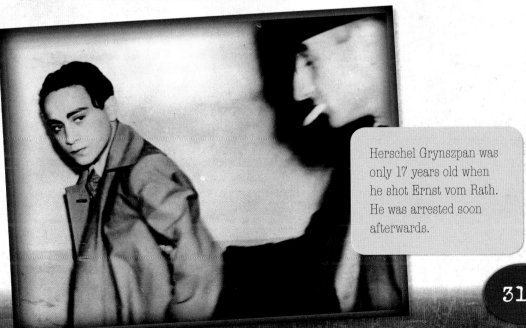

Herschel Grynszpan was only 17 years old when he shot Ernst vom Rath. He was arrested soon afterwards.

Hatred and vengeance

The attack on Ernst vom Rath was the spark the Nazis had been waiting for. They had separated the Jews from ordinary society and whipped up a frenzy of hatred against them. Yet the majority of Germans had still not become involved with anti-Semitic actions. This attack was an opportunity to turn the Nazis' hatred into a nationwide desire for revenge – something bigger and more destructive than ever before.

The Nazis made the most of it. On the morning of 8 November, the newspapers branded the Jewish people as murderers. The government announced punishments for all Jews, which included closing down Jewish newspapers and magazines and barring Jewish children from Aryan elementary schools. Party activists organized anti-Jewish riots. That night, a synagogue was burned down and shops were looted. In the new prison camp at Buchenwald, at least 70 Jews were executed.[6]

The pogrom is approved

Vom Rath died of his wounds during the afternoon of 9 November. Nazi anger at the Jewish people grew more intense, although some Nazis complained that the German population was not taking much notice of events. Hitler was told of vom Rath's death that evening. He was in Munich at a dinner to celebrate the 15th anniversary of his 1923 putsch attempt (see page 11). Goebbels suggested that Nazi storm troopers should lead and encourage protests against the Jews throughout Germany. Hitler is reported as saying, "The SA should be allowed to have a fling."[7]

The conversation with Goebbels seems to be the only direct action that Hitler took. He did not plan the massive night of violence, but he gave his approval for it. Even at this stage, he was anxious not to appear personally involved with violent anti-Jewish actions. If the pogrom failed, he would be blamed, and this would have damaged his image as an infallible (perfect) leader.

Decisive words: Hitler's approval

"I explain the matter to the Führer. He decides: let the demonstrations continue. Pull back the police. The Jews should for once get to feel the anger of the people."[9]

Joseph Goebbels, record of his conversation with Adolf Hitler, recorded in his diary on 9 November 1938

In October 1938 thousands of Polish-born Jews were expelled from Germany. Poland refused to allow them entry, so they were stranded on the border. Many were forced to live in stables and other farm buildings, with no heating and little food.

Instead, Hitler left it to Goebbels to make a rabble-rousing speech instructing Nazi leaders about what should be done. They then left, ready to pass the orders on to the storm troopers and party members who were going to lead the action on the streets. Hitler made just one other decision that evening. He called Himmler and told him to keep the SS in their barracks. This was a night for uncontrolled anarchy (lawlessness), not the methodical brutality that was the SS speciality.[8]

"Working towards the Führer"

Adolf Hitler was the unquestioned leader of the Nazis. But he did not make every decision or shape every piece of government policy. Increasingly, he left the everyday running of affairs in Germany to ministers such as Goebbels and Himmler and to officials lower down the chain of command. All were expected to understand what he wanted. Back in 1934, Nazi politician Werner Willikens explained this. People should not wait for orders, he said: "Rather, it is the duty of every single person to attempt, in the spirit of the Führer, to work towards him. The one who works correctly towards the Führer along his lines and towards his aim ... will have the finest reward."[10]

Storm of destruction

On 9 November, when news arrived in Berlin that Ernst vom Rath had died, German radio stations observed a two-minute silence in his memory. The official Nazi reaction began at about 10.30 in the evening.[11] Party leaders in Munich and Berlin, including Reinhard Heydrich, summoned local bands of activists or SA storm troopers and ordered them to start "demonstrations" against the Jews.

These bands rampaged through the streets, breaking windows with bricks and clubs, beating up Jewish people, and handing out leaflets that said: "Führer! Free us from the Jewish plague!"[12] They burned down synagogues and destroyed holy Jewish texts. They smashed Jewish properties and stole or destroyed anything of value. This attracted mixed reaction from Germans. Some joined in the wild looting, and the police were instructed not to interfere; others were shocked by the violence. They did not necessarily think that Jewish people should be treated in the same way as other Germans, but thought the state should solve the "Jewish question" in an "orderly" manner.

Reinhard Heydrich 1904–1942

Born: Halle, Germany

Role: SS general, Gestapo chief, and architect of the **Holocaust**

Reinhard Heydrich came from a wealthy family. He joined the SS in 1931, and soon became head of gathering intelligence (secret information). One of the Nazi Party's most extreme anti-Semites, he was one of the main organizers of Kristallnacht, and later of the mass murder of Jews. Cold and ruthless, he was described by Hitler as "the man with the iron heart."[13]

Did you know? Heydrich was fatally injured in Prague in May 1942 when Czech resistance fighters trained in Britain rolled a grenade under his vehicle.

The same thing happened in more than 1,000 cities, towns, and villages throughout Germany, Austria, and the Sudeten territory. In many places, Himmler allowed some SS men to join the activists, although they had to wear civilian clothes rather than their uniforms. Armed with sledgehammers, clubs, and cans of petrol, these Nazi gangs moved through the streets. Many carried lists of Jewish addresses.

Shattered glass covered the streets outside smashed Jewish shops after Kristallnacht. Some Germans found the sight something to smile at.

Eyewitnesses

The attacks and lootings went on through the night and until 5 o'clock in the evening the next day. The following are some personal accounts by people who witnessed the violence.

"A group of men, some in brown uniforms, were screaming insults and beating with no mercy. The younger brother of my classmate was tied to a bicycle by his neck and had to run after the bicycle so as not to be choked."[15]

Joseph Schwarzburg

"As we reached the synagogue, flames began to rise from one end of the building. The crowd surged forward and greedy hands tore seats and woodwork from the building to feed the flames. We saw a section of the mob start off along the road where granite cubes had been heaped. Youths, men, and women, howling deliriously, hurled the blocks through the windows and at the closed doors. In a few minutes the doors gave way and the mob, shouting and fighting, surged inside to pillage and loot."[14]

Michael Bruce, an Englishman (non-Jewish)

"My father opened [the door] and I saw three Nazis standing there. They looked big, and were carrying axes, hammers and saws. They pushed us aside and began to destroy everything in our house. When everything was broken, they pushed my father and my grandfather down the stairs. I was screaming and pulling on my father's sleeve... They were taken away... I learnt later that the men were taken to Dachau."[16]

Lea Weems

The cost of Kristallnacht

When the mayhem ended, the wrecking of Jewish communities was complete. Homes had been smashed up, their belongings stolen, their few remaining businesses destroyed, and their synagogues burned. Much worse still, a huge number of Jewish men had been arrested by the Gestapo, to shock their families into leaving Germany. The men were sent to concentration camps, where they were forced to do hard labour. There, they faced torture, starvation, and sudden death. Those left behind (mostly those who were old or ill) lived in terror and poverty.

But the Nazis added more humiliation. On 10 November, Hitler told Goebbels he had decided the Jews would have to clean up the mess – even though they were the victims. They would also have to repair damage to their property with their own money. Finally, the Jewish people must pay a fine as punishment for the destruction. Goering fixed this fine at a massive 1 billion reichsmark (the currency at the time) – the equivalent of about £255 million today.[17]

Kristallnacht in figures

The following statistics show the damage done during the events of Kristallnacht:

German Jews killed 91

Jewish men sent to prison camps . . . 30,000

Jewish businesses destroyed. 7,500

Synagogues destroyed . . . . .276[21]

Value of the damage done
. . . . 49.5 million reichsmark
. . . .(£3.9 million at 1938 values)[22]

People in the United States were outraged at the events. On 23 November, there were mass demonstrations in New York and Washington, DC, against the Nazi atrocities, and two days later protesters in Chicago burnt German flags.[18] US President Franklin D. Roosevelt said: "I could scarcely believe that such things could occur in a 20th-century civilization."[19]

The reaction was just as strong in Europe. Politicians and journalists in Britain and France, as well as those on Germany's western borders, such as Switzerland and Holland, condemned the violence. A British diplomat, George Ogilvie-Forbes, wrote that Germany's Jews were "not a national but a world problem which if neglected contains the seeds of a terrible vengeance".[20] But governments took little action.

Jewish shopkeepers were forced to clear up the rubble and glass fragments outside their looted shops.

The effect on Nazi policy

The events of Kristallnacht marked a turning point in the treatment of the German Jews. It started as an organized campaign of terror and revenge. For the first time, the Nazis made clear that they were willing to kill large numbers of people to get their message across. Measures taken after the riots (including the "atonement fine") sucked away Jews' remaining wealth and excluded them almost completely from German society.

Kristallnacht also showed that pogroms of this kind were no longer useful. Some Nazi leaders, such as Goering, were angry at the wild violence and the huge amount of damage caused. Many ordinary Germans were shocked by what they had seen. This was not the order and stability they had hoped Hitler would bring. Hitler realized that brutal chaos – with thugs on the street, smashed windows, and burning synagogues – was not a very effective way of getting rid of the Jews. He felt that a different system had to be found.

What do you think?

What did Hitler gain?

Did Hitler gain anything from the events of Kristallnacht? The **atrocity** caused a lot of damage and drew condemnation from other countries. Would the Nazis have developed their **extermination** programme anyway without it? Do some research and see what you think. Look, for example, at: www.historyplace.com/worldwar2/triumph/tr-knacht.htm.

37

Holocaust

In a speech on 30 January 1939, Hitler repeated his fixed belief that the Jews were the biggest threat to world peace, saying: "If international finance Jewry inside and outside Europe should succeed in plunging the nations once more into a world war, the result will not be the victory of Jewry, but the annihilation [complete destruction] of the Jewish race in Europe!"[1]

A new world war

In fact, it was the Germans who plunged the world into the next world war. Hitler was confident that the major European powers would not stand against him, and so he continued his expansion east. On 15 March, his troops took over the remainder of Czechoslovakia. A triumphant Hitler boasted: "This is the happiest day of my life!"[2] Britain and France did nothing in response.

The Nazis' next target was Poland. Hitler's plan was horribly simple: to massacre large numbers of Poles and settle the

The Einsatzgruppen

The Einsatzgruppen (meaning "Task Forces") were special SS units that Heydrich formed in 1938. They were mobile killing parties that were first used in the conquests of Czechoslovakia and Poland. The job of the Einsatzgruppen was to follow the invading forces and murder all those defined as racial or political opponents. This meant Jewish people in particular. Victims were usually shot and buried in mass graves.

country with Germans. On 23 August, he signed an agreement with the Soviet Union declaring that the two states would not fight each other, but rather would divide Poland between them. On 1 September, German forces crossed the border into Poland. Two days later, Britain and France declared war on Germany. World War II had begun.

The Jews of Poland

There were now only about 350,000 Jews left in Germany and Austria. Since Kristallnacht, the number of emigrants had doubled in a year to 80,000.[3] But Hitler's conquests brought another huge Jewish population under German control. A third of all Europe's Jews (over 3.25 million) lived in Poland.[4] As the German army smashed its way across the Polish landscape, the Nazis developed new and more brutal anti-Semitic measures.

At this stage, the Nazis had three main systems:

- *Slave labour*: Jews in prison camps were forced to work hard in appalling conditions. Many died of exhaustion or starvation.

- *Forced emigration*: Jews were scared into emigration by persecution. Some were also forcibly moved into neighbouring countries.

- *Concentration*: Many Jews were trapped in small areas of towns. These were called **ghettos**. The men arrested after Kristallnacht were confined to concentration camps.

Another new element involved the Einsatzgruppen SS units, which detained and killed any Poles defined as "undesirable". These included communists, politicians, and Roma, as well as Jews. In the first few weeks of the war, more than 30,000 people, including more than 5,000 Jews, were murdered. But this did little to solve what the Nazis saw as the massive Jewish problem.[5] Nazi leaders thought of new ways to get rid of them.

Jewish prisoners were forced to dig their own graves bofore they were shot by the Einsatzgruppen.

Advancing west and east

By the end of June 1940, Germany had gained astounding success. Most of mainland Europe had been conquered, and the United States had remained neutral. Britain was the only major enemy still fighting. By June 1941, German forces had swept through Yugoslavia and Greece and landed in North Africa.

At this point, Hitler made his biggest gamble. On 22 June, he turned against his Soviet allies and invaded Russia. From the start, this was a more shockingly savage campaign than ever before. As the Nazis drove towards the Russian capital, Moscow, they killed not just enemy soldiers, but also whole communities. Anyone who resisted was massacred. And, of course, the terror was aimed at the Russian Jews.

A trail of blood

The Nazi killing machine was now hard at work. In Poland and the Soviet Union, the SS and other agencies shot, hanged, and worked or beat to death vast numbers of people. Over 2 million Soviet prisoners of war and 1 million Jews died in this way.[6]

In Warsaw, Poland, Jews could only get from one part of the ghetto to another by crossing a footbridge. The street below was only for the use of Aryans.

Decisive words: Hitler's prophecy

"The Führer is resolved to make a clean sweep. He prophesied to the Jews that if they were to bring about another world war, they would bring about their own destruction as a result. This was not empty talk. The world war is here, the destruction of the Jews must be the necessary consequence."[12]

Adolf Hitler, from a speech on 12 December 1941, reported by Joseph Goebbels in his diary

Meanwhile, the Germans were establishing more of what became over 1,000 Jewish ghettos in Eastern Europe.[7] These were areas of cities where Jews were forced to live in overcrowded conditions. The biggest was in Warsaw, where 400,000 Polish Jews were crammed into a tiny area ringed with walls and wire.[8]

The "Final Solution"

On 31 July 1941, Goering wrote to Heydrich, ordering him "to carry out all the necessary preparations with regard to organizational and financial matters for bringing about a final solution of the Jewish question".[9] There were no precise details that describe plans for an organized policy of killing, but the phrase "Final Solution" has since become a standard description of the next stage of the extermination of the Jews.

During that summer and autumn, Nazi scientists and engineers developed a new method of mass murder using poison gas. This would be quicker and cheaper than shooting. The first extermination camp began operating at Kulmhof, and the first gassings took place on 27 October, when more than 100 Jewish patients in an old people's home in Kalisz, Poland, were loaded into trucks. Exhaust fumes were piped into the trucks, killing them.[10] In November, senior Nazi official Alfred Rosenberg announced that "the biological extermination of all Jews in Europe" had begun.[11]

Euthanasia and the gas chambers

In 1939, the Nazis began a programme of euthanasia, in which old or handicapped people were put painlessly to death. The aim was to keep the Aryan race perfect and healthy. As this would involve the deaths of thousands, scientists looked for efficient methods of murder. By 1940, they had devised the first use of gas chambers, in which victims were suffocated or poisoned by gas. This method was later developed for mass killings of Jews.[13]

Factories of death

On 20 January 1942, leading Nazi officials (though not Hitler) met at Wannsee, near Berlin. There they discussed details of the "Final Solution." At this point, Germany seemed less certain to conquer the territory needed for deporting the Jewish population, so the subject had suddenly become more urgent. Heydrich was anxious to take control and speed up action against the Jewish people. He outlined plans to deport them all to Eastern Europe. State Secretary Joseph Bühler demanded that "preliminary measures for the final solution should immediately be taken".[14]

"Preliminary measures" may have referred to a policy of shootings or expulsion across the border into the occupied Soviet Union. It may have referred to building extermination camps. But the shortage of territory for deportation meant that new solutions were explored and mass killing became the chosen option.

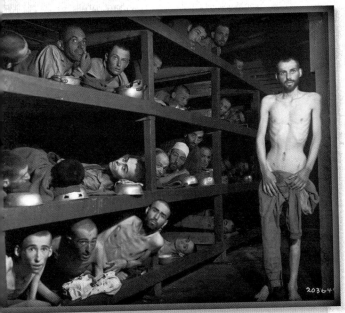

Male inmates of extermination camps were starved, beaten, or overworked to death. These survivors at Buchenwald were photographed when the camp was liberated by the Allies in 1945.

The development of gas chambers already marked a new and even more horrific stage in Jewish genocide. Poland now became the centre of the killing. Enormous new death camps were opened at Auschwitz, Treblinka, Belzec, Sobibor, and Majdanek. They were laid out to make the killing as quick and efficient as possible, with railway platforms and large gas chambers nearby.

At some camps with work facilities, the victims were split up on arrival. Healthier prisoners were retained for activities that helped the war effort, such as hard labour, while the rest were usually sent directly to the chambers. Stripped of clothes and belongings,

Prisoers who avoided the gas chambers were put to work. These men at Sachsenhausen sewed and mended clothing.

they were gassed. By mid-1942, a poison gas called Zyklon-B was introduced at Auschwitz, instead of carbon monoxide (a poisonous gas) from vehicle exhausts. Afterwards, the corpses were burned.

Hitler defeated

In 1941, both the United States and the Soviet Union entered the war, and this greatly changed the course of the conflict. Their huge manpower and resources of weapons gradually proved to be too strong for the Germans (and for the Japanese, who had joined hostilities at the same time). By 1943, Hitler's Russian invasion ended in disaster.

In 1944, **Allied** troops landed in Normandy, France (an event known as D-Day). As British and US forces advanced into Germany from the west, the Soviet Red Army advanced from the east. By mid-April 1945, the Red Army had begun the final attack on Berlin. Hitler committed suicide in his bunker there on 30 April. The remaining Nazi leaders finally surrendered on 8 May. World War II was over.

Hiding the evidence

Gassings stopped in November 1944, partly because the Nazis wanted to destroy the evidence.[15] Some camps were demolished, and victims' remains were buried. The Nazis tried to stop their prisoners from falling into Allied hands. Thousands were forced on death marches to camps inside Germany.[16] But other camps remained open. Auschwitz was **liberated** by Soviet troops on 27 January 1945. Dachau was liberated by US troops on 29 April.[17]

43

Hitler's legacy

Adolf Hitler's thirst for power led him to become the leader of Germany in 1933. This gave the Nazis the opportunity to put their extreme policies into practice. Hitler's fanatical hatred of the Jews and his crusade for the racial cleansing of his country led to Kristallnacht in 1938. His decision to conquer Europe and expand German "living space" to the East led to the outbreak of World War II and the nightmare of what we now call the Holocaust.

The legacy for the Jews

So, the most obvious **legacy** of Hitler's rule is the enormous list of Jews who died in pogroms, ghettos, massacres by firing squads, forced labour camps, and gas chambers (see the box below for these numbers). The pre-war European Jewish population was about 9 million; the total of the dead was almost 6 million. Of these, more than 1 million were children.[1] Few of the victims left diaries or letters behind, so we know very little about exactly what happened to most of them.

Besides the dead, there were the survivors. Those who were fortunate enough to escape the death camps had often lost everything – family, friends, possessions, communities, and livelihoods. Many were also among the millions of refugees who had been displaced by the fighting and were homeless. Most were unable or unwilling to return to their native lands, where they had been persecuted.

How many Jews were murdered?

The exact total of the Jews who were murdered will never be known. Here are the minimum numbers, although the true figures could be much higher:

Country....Number of dead	Country....Number of dead	Country....Number of dead
Austria 50,000	Greece 60,000	Poland 2,900,000
Belgium 28,000	Hungary 550,000	Romania. 271,000
Bohemia/Moravia .78,000	Latvia 70,000	Slovakia 68,000
France. 77,000	Lithuania 140,000	Soviet Union. . . 1,000,000
Germany. 135,000	Netherlands 100,000	Yugoslavia 56,000
		Other 13,000

TOTAL: 5,596,000[3]

When World War II ended in 1945, Allied ships carried Jewish survivors of Nazi persecution to a new life in Palestine.

The Holocaust and the continued plight of the Jewish refugees led to the foundation of Israel. Before the war, many Jews had already emigrated to Palestine. In May 1948, British control of Palestine ended, and it was decided that a homeland would be established there for all Jewish people. The country was divided into two states: one for Jews and one for Palestinian Arabs. By 1950, there were over 1 million Jews in the new state of Israel.

The founding of Israel angered neighbouring states, which believed it had robbed the Palestinian Arabs of their own homeland. Five Arab countries launched an invasion in 1948, to destroy the new state. It failed, but there have been several more wars between the two sides. The violence continues today.

Allied governments had known much about the Holocaust, but the revelations in the decades after the war stunned the wider population. As the full truth about the genocide emerged, people were confronted with a horror on an unheard-of scale. This growing understanding led to many changes in social attitudes, especially the breakdown of institutionalized anti-Semitism in many countries.

Today, there are thriving Jewish communities in many parts of the world. By far the largest of these are in Israel (5.7 million) and in the United States (5.2 million).[2] The US Jewish community has been particularly successful. It has had a distinctive and far-reaching impact on politics, industry, the arts and sciences, and many other areas of modern life.

Germany: the economic and social legacy

Germany ended World War II with a shattered economy and its towns, agriculture, and industry destroyed by bombs and shells. A total of 7.7 million German soldiers and civilians had died during the conflict.[4] The country lost all the territory it had gained in the war, and about 20 per cent of its pre-war territory as well. Returning refugees and prisoners of war found poverty, starvation, disease, and despair.

The German people had no power to govern themselves. After the final surrender in World War II, Germany itself was divided into four zones. Each of these was controlled by one of the major Allies: the Soviet Union, the United States, Britain, and France. In 1949, two German governments were formed, one in the West, one in the East.

The victorious nations helped to rebuild the German economy and its wrecked infrastructure of transport and buildings. They also made sure that the country was "de-Nazified" by removing surviving Nazis from key positions. This was deliberately structured to prevent the loss of those whose skills would speed the economic recovery.

Only obeying orders

Many leading Nazis excused their deeds by claiming to obey Hitler's wishes. Here are some of their words:

> "Who is a little man like me to trouble his head about it? All we knew was obedience to orders."[8]
>
> *SS officer Adolf Eichmann (on killing Jews)*

> "I have no conscience. My conscience is Adolf Hitler."[9]
>
> *Hermann Goering*

The legacy of shame

Soon after the war ended, an unknown person painted in huge letters on a wall in Munich the simple words: "I am ashamed to be a German."[5] The German nation had to bear the huge weight of guilt. This was partly for the massive death and destruction of the fighting, but mainly for the horrendous atrocity of the Holocaust. "A thousand years will pass and this guilt of Germany will not be erased," wrote Hans Frank, who had been Hitler's governor of Poland.[6] Many Germans still carry the burden of that shame today, although of course they have developed into a very different kind of society.

Several surviving Nazi leaders were tried for war crimes at Nuremberg in 1946. Among them was Hermann Goering (middle row, seated left). He killed himself before he could be executed.

Who took the blame?

Hans Frank was one of several Nazi officials who were executed after being tried for war crimes in Nuremberg in 1946. Others committed suicide or were imprisoned. Many received only light punishment and lived long lives or escaped from Europe and hid themselves in friendly countries such as Paraguay in South America. Few who were questioned showed any remorse or shame.[7]

Nazi hunters

After the war, many leading Nazis fled abroad and lived with new names and identities. Several people and organizations dedicated their lives to tracking them down. These "Nazi hunters" have brought many notable war criminals to justice. One of their most famous successes was when Israeli agents kidnapped Adolf Eichmann from Argentina in 1960. Eichmann, one of the major architects of the Holocaust, was tried and executed in Israel in 1962.[10]

But how did ordinary Germans feel? A large number of people had certainly been involved in the crimes of the Nazi state – civil servants, businessmen, the armed forces, and some church leaders. Many others acknowledged their guilt, but some claimed they did not realize what was happening in Nazi Germany. Some knew about the persecution and killing of Jews but were afraid to oppose it.

The legacy for the world

World War II was the greatest disaster of the 20th century. The Holocaust was one of the worst atrocities in all of history. Today, we link these two events with one man: Adolf Hitler. He led his nation into a war that ruined it and that killed at least 50 million people.[11] He inspired his followers to attempt to wipe out the entire Jewish population in Europe.

However, the death of Hitler in 1945 marked the end of an era in world history. Germany had been very powerful since it had become a unified nation in 1871. In all that time, it had tried to dominate Europe, and for this reason had started two world wars. Its aggressive policies and drive for expansion had led to several major conflicts, most notably two ruinous world wars. After 1945, Germany was a very different country, at first divided in two. It eventually regained its economic power, but it also became a leading member of peaceful international organizations such as the United Nations and the European Union.

The United Nations

The United Nations (UN) was created at the end of World War II, in 1945. Almost every sovereign (independent) state in the world is a member. The UN's main aims are to encourage global harmony, to uphold human rights, and to help the development of poorer countries. The Security Council of the UN works to maintain international peace and security. The UN headquarters are in New York City, USA.

The Iron Curtain

World War II changed the political map of Europe. The massive advance of the Red Army from Russia gave the Soviet Union control over most of Eastern Europe. The Soviets imposed and controlled communist governments there, creating a giant "bloc" of states tightly ruled from Moscow. Free travel was no longer possible between East and West. Europe, like Germany itself, was divided in two.

In 1946, British Prime Minister Winston Churchill described this division as an "Iron Curtain" across the continent. On one side was the communist eastern bloc. On the other were the free **capitalist** nations of the West, which pledged (along with the

United States) to resist the spread of communism. This led to a long period of tension, with both sides building up stocks of nuclear weapons, that was known as the Cold War (because there were no direct battles). It only ended when the Soviet Union broke up in 1991.

Guarding against fascism

The Nazis are considered heroes to a small minority of right-wing activists and anti-Semites throughout the world. Some dispute the details of the Holocaust, and a few even deny that it really happened. For example, in 2005, Iran's president, Mahmoud Ahmadinejad, called the Holocaust a "myth".[12] In 2009, British Catholic Bishop Richard Williamson denied the existence of the gas chambers.[13]

However, the horror of the Holocaust has also changed the way people look at society. It forced them to be more aware of later acts of genocide throughout the world, and to understand better the roots of racism and racial violence. The Holocaust deaths are regularly remembered, especially on 27 January each year (the date when Auschwitz was liberated). The United Nations has made this International Commemoration Day for Victims of the Holocaust.

The biggest Nazi extermination camp was at Auschwitz in Poland. It has been preserved as a museum to commemorate the thousands who died there.

What if?

Adolf Hitler was chiefly responsible for the Holocaust and World War II, bringing death and destruction that changed the world forever. But what would have happened if he had made different decisions? Or what would have happened if other world leaders had acted differently? How different might the course of history have been? And would many millions of lives have been saved? Here are just a few of those possible turning points.

What if Hitler was opposed more forcefully?

Hitler defied international opinion throughout the 1930s, relying on forcefulness and lies to get his way. His occupation (taking over) of neighbouring territories and growing anti-Semitic terror outraged many foreign leaders. But they failed to take any action. Threats of military force or economic sanctions might have stopped the Nazis' advance towards world war and genocide.

What if Hitler had stopped it?

Hitler could have forbidden the nationwide violence of Kristallnacht. But would this have changed the fate of the Jewish people?

There were many failed attempts to assassinate Hitler. One of the last was a bomb that wrecked his headquarters at Rastenburg in 1944. Italian dictator Benito Mussolini (left) joined Hitler to inspect the damage.

Kristallnacht was a stark demonstration to the world of how the Nazis intended to treat the Jews. It also encouraged other countries, such as Britain, to continue rearming and to resist Nazi territorial aggression. But even without it, the Holocaust would probably still have occurred, because the Nazis would have faced the same challenges in finding more territory to send its Jewish population to.

What if Hitler had not invaded Russia?

In the spring of 1941, Hitler ruled almost all of Europe. He had failed to invade a weakened Britain. Instead, he decided in June to turn east and send his troops into the vast territories of the Soviet Union. His troops became trapped by the harsh weather and the huge Russian Army. If Hitler had not done this, he could perhaps have conquered Britain and dominated Europe for a very long time.

What if Pearl Harbor had never happened?

On 7 December 1941, Japanese planes attacked the US fleet in Pearl Harbor, Hawaii. As a result, Japan's ally Germany declared war on the United States. But the vast supply of US soldiers and weapons would have a major effect on defeating Germany. This had nothing to do with Hitler's decision-making, of course, but if Pearl Harbor had never happened, the United States might have stayed neutral, Germany might have won, and the Holocaust would have gone on uninterrupted.

Did the Holocaust lose Germany the war?

The Nazis developed the horrendous system of death camps to exterminate an entire race as quickly as possible. But, apart from the unspeakable suffering involved, the operation of that system needed about 250,000 soldiers and other officials, and relatively few other resources.[1] These would not have made a significant difference to the course of the war.

What do you think?

Find out more

On these pages, there are a number of ideas about how different decisions might have changed history. Do you agree with the suggested answers to the "What if?" questions? Or do you have a better response? Select one of the topics here to study further. You will need to do more research first. Here is one website with general news and features about Hitler and the Holocaust that may help you get started:

www.spartacus.schoolnet.co.uk/GERhitler.htm

The road to genocide

"I will go down as the greatest German in history!" boasted Hitler in March 1939.[1] In fact, he is remembered as the most hated German in history. This is not just because he pushed the world into World War II, the largest and most disastrous of all wars. It is also because his ferocious hatred of the Jews inspired the Holocaust, one of the most monstrous atrocities in history.

Corporal to dictator

Hitler blamed the Jews for Germany's defeat in World War I. He was already an obsessive anti-Semite and made this hatred one of the driving forces of the newly formed Nazi Party in the 1920s. Using violence to silence opponents, and his own brilliant gift for giving speeches, he led the party to power in 1933, when he became German chancellor.

Aided by other committed Jew-haters, such as Goebbels and Himmler, Hitler quickly turned Germany into a dictatorship and began a programme of anti-Semitic persecution. He also expanded the national armed forces and seized control of neighbouring countries to the east, including Austria and parts of Czechoslovakia. British and French leaders were eager to avoid another war, so they did not oppose him.

International Holocaust Remembrance Day is held on 27 January every year. Death camp survivors lay wreaths of flowers and say prayers in the Auschwitz camp.

Kristallnacht

By 1938, the Nazis were increasing pressure on German Jews to emigrate, seizing their property and branding them as outsiders. Beatings and mass violence by storm troopers and other party members were widespread. The shooting of a German official by a Polish-born Jew on 6 November provided the excuse for violent anti-Jewish demonstrations, which became known as Kristallnacht. Approved by Hitler, but organized by Goebbels, Heydrich, and others, the wave of attacks began on Jewish shops, synagogues, and homes. Over 90 Jews were killed, and many buildings were destroyed, littering pavements with fragments of glass. At least 30,000 Jewish men were arrested and sent to prison camps.

Kristallnacht did not mark the real beginning of the Holocaust. But, for the first time, brutal persecution of the Jews, including massive force and killing was given official backing, and there were mass arrests. What was Hitler's true role in Kristallnacht? He had merely given his permission for the violence, preferring not to associate himself with direct anti-Semitic action.

All the same, the persecution suited his policies. When wartime events meant that emigration was no longer practical, other Nazi leaders went on to devise the death camps as an efficient tool of genocide during 1941, and Hitler must have approved. Even though he never visited a death camp or learnt the technical details of a gas chamber, he knew that his followers were fulfilling his vision of a Jew-free Europe. This was his most enduring legacy.

What do you think?

Are there any positive outcomes?

The Holocaust ended nearly 70 years ago. A huge amount of evidence has since been gathered and judgments have been made. So, looking back to 1945, do you think there have been any positive outcomes of this appalling event? You may find this distressing to think about, but here are some suggestions:

- The foundation and growth of Israel as a homeland for the world's Jews

- Increased global awareness of the evils of racial discrimination and violence

Timeline

1919

September
Adolf Hitler joins the German Workers' Party (GWP)

1920

24 February
The GWP is relaunched as the Nazi Party, with Hitler as its leader

1920

October
The Sturmabteilung (SA) is formed

1921

9 November
Hitler makes first major speech for the Nazis in Munich, attacking the Jews

1923

9 November
Hitler leads an attempted putsch in Munich

1938

13 March
Germany completes the Anschluss with Austria

1936

1 August
The Berlin Olympics begin

1936

7 March
The German army enters the Rhineland

1933

28 April
Goering forms the Gestapo

1938

10 October
German troops march into the Sudetenland after the Munich Agreement with Britain and France

1938

27 October
Polish-born Jews are removed from Germany

1938

6 November
Herschel Grynszpan shoots Ernst vom Rath

1938

9–10 November
Kristallnacht takes place, with widespread violence against Jews

1944

6 June
D-Day: The Allies launch an invasion of France

1943

8 September
Italy surrenders to the Allies

1943

31 January
German forces surrender to the Soviets at Stalingrad

1942

6 November
The Allies defeat the Germans at El Alamein, North Africa

1942

6 June
The United States defeats the Japanese navy at Midway, which is a turning point in the war in the Pacific

1944

20 June
An assassination plot against Hitler fails

1944

November
The gassing programme stops in death camps

1945

27 January
The Red Army liberates the Auschwitz death camp

1945

22 April
The Red Army enters Berlin

1945

29 April
US troops liberate Dachau

1924

20 December
Hitler leaves
Landsberg
Prison

1925

June
The
Schutzstaffel
(SS) is formed

1925

July
Mein Kampf
is published
for the
first time

1928

November
Goebbels
becomes head
of propaganda
for the Nazis

1932

27 January
Hitler makes a
key speech to
industrialists in
Düsseldorf, which
gains their support
for the Nazis

1933

7 April
Jews are
dismissed from
German civil
service jobs

1933

1 April
A national
boycott of
Jewish shops
begins

1933

20 March
The first
concentration
camp at Dachau
opens

1933

27 February
The Reichstag
catches fire;
Hitler dissolves
parliament

1933

30 January
Hitler is
appointed
chancellor of
Germany

1939

3 September
Britain and
France
declare war
on Germany

1940

May/June
Germany invades the
Low Countries (modern
Belgium, Luxembourg,
and the Netherlands),
Scandinavia, and France

1940

October
The Nazis
establish a
Jewish ghetto
in Warsaw

1941

Summer
The first mass
deportations
of Jews to
death camps in
Poland occur

1941

22 June
Hitler launches
an invasion
of the Soviet
Union

1942

20 January
Nazi leaders
meet at
Wannsee to
decide how
to deal with
European Jews

1941

12 December
Hitler again
predicts the
destruction of the
Jews of Europe,
this time in a
speech in Berlin

1941

8 December
Germany
declares war
on the US
following the
Japanese attack
on Pearl Harbor

1941

27 October
Gassing of
Jewish civilians
takes place in
Kalisz, Poland

1941

31 July
Goering
mentions a
"Final Solution"
in a letter to
Heydrich

1945

30 April
Hitler commits
suicide

1945

8 May
Germany
surrenders,
leading to
Victory in
Europe Day

1945

15 August
Japan surrenders,
leading to Victory
Over Japan Day;
World War II ends

1946

1 October
Verdicts are announced at
end of Nuremberg War Trials
The International Military
War Tribunal at Nuremberg
announces its verdict

Notes on sources

A night of broken glass (pages 4–5)

1. US Holocaust Memorial Museum, "Kristallnacht: A Nationwide Pogrom, November 9–10, 1938", http://www.ushmm.org/wlc/en/article.php?ModuleId=10005201.

2. Martin Gilbert, *Kristallnacht: Prelude to Destruction* (London: Harper Perennial, 2007), 41.

The Jews of Europe (pages 6–9)

1. Klaus P. Fischer, *The History of an Obsession: German Judeophobia and the Holocaust* (New York: Continuum, 1998), 33.

2. *Ibid.*, 34.

3. *Ibid.*, 29.

4. Edward H. Flannery, *The Anguish of the Jews: Twenty-Three Centuries of Anti-Semitism* (Mahwah, N.J.: Paulist Press, 2004), 158.

5. Fischer, *The History of an Obsession*, 124.

6. Martin Gilbert, *The Holocaust: The Jewish Tragedy* (London: Collins, 1986), 21–22.

7. Ian Kershaw, *Hitler, 1889–1936: Hubris* (New York: W. W. Norton, 1999), 87.

8. Jewish Virtual Library, "Adolf Hitler's First Antisemitic Writing", http://www.jewishvirtuallibrary.org/jsource/Holocaust/Adolf_Hitler%27s_First_Antisemitic_Writing.html.

Hitler's rise to power (pages 10–15)

1. Gilbert, *The Holocaust*, 23.

2. *Ibid.*, 24.

3. *Ibid.*, 258.

4. *Ibid.*

5. William L. Shirer, *The Rise and Fall of the Third Reich: A History of Nazi Germany* (London: Secker & Warburg, 1959), 119.

6. *Ibid.*, 120.

7. Kershaw, *Hitler, 1889–1936: Hubris*, 277.

8. *Ibid.*, 404.

9. Shirer, *The Rise and Fall of the Third Reich*, 138.

10. *Ibid.*, 166.

The persecution begins (pages 16–23)

1. Kershaw, *Hitler, 1889–1936: Hubris*, 441.

2. *Ibid.*, 460.

3. Peter Longerich, *Holocaust: The Nazi Persecution and the Murder of the Jews* (Oxford: Oxford University Press, 2010), 33.

4. Gilbert, *The Holocaust*, 33.

5. Fischer, *The History of an Obsession*, 229.

6. Gilbert, *The Holocaust*, 34.

7. *Ibid.*, 36.

8. Longerich, *Holocaust*, 44.

9. *Ibid.*, 46.

10. Kershaw, *Hitler, 1889–1936: Hubris*, 492.

11. *Ibid.*, 517.

12. Fischer, *The History of an Obsession*, 206.

The Nazi grip tightens (pages 24–29)

1. Ian Kershaw, *Hitler, 1936-1945: Nemesis* (London: Allen Lane, 2000), 1.

2. Longerich, *Holocaust*, 63.

3. *Ibid.*, 69.

4. Gilbert, *The Holocaust*, 55.

5. M. Hughes, "The Banality of Brutality: British Armed Forces and the Repression of the Arab Revolt in Palestine, 1936–39", *English Historical Review*, vol. 124, no. 507 (2009), 314–54.

6. Gilbert, *The Holocaust*, 58.

7. *Ibid.*, 60.

8. Kershaw, *Hitler, 1936–1945: Nemesis*, 134.

Decision time (pages 30–37)

1. Kershaw, *Hitler, 1936–1945: Nemesis*, 135.

2. *Ibid.*, 136.

3. US Holocaust Memorial Museum, "Germany: Jewish Population in 1933", http://www.ushmm.org/wlc/en/article.php?ModuleId=10005276.

4. Aubrey Boag, "They Expected the Worst – They Did Not Expect the Unthinkable: Jewish Emigration from Germany, 1933–1941", UCSB Department of History, http://www.history.ucsb.edu/faculty/marcuse/classes/133b/07Projects/BoagJewishEmigration074.htm.

5. Gilbert, *The Holocaust*, 64.

6. Gilbert, *Kristallnacht*, 27.

7. Fischer, *The History of an Obsession*, 281.

8. Kershaw, *Hitler, 1936–1945: Nemesis*, 139.

9. Ian Kershaw, *Hitler 1936-1945: Nemesis*, 138.

10. Kershaw, *Hitler, 1889–1936: Hubris*, 529.

11. *Ibid.*, 138.

12. Gilbert, *Kristallnacht*, 29.

13. The History Place, "SS Leader Reinhard Heydrich", http://www.historyplace.com/worldwar2/biographies/heydrich-biography.htm.

14. Simon Wiesenthal Centre, "Kristallnacht+70: Night of Broken Glass", http://www.wiesenthal.com/atf/cf/%7BDFD2AAC1-2ADE-428A-9263-35234229D8D8%7D/KRISTALLNACHT.PDF.

15. *Ibid.*, 87.

16. *Ibid.*, 113–14.

17. Kershaw, *Hitler, 1936–1945: Nemesis*, 143–45.

18. Gilbert, *The Holocaust*, 74.

19. Fischer, *The History of an Obsession*, 283.

20. Gilbert, *The Holocaust*, 74.

21. Fischer, *The History of an Obsession*, 282.

22. Longerich, *Holocaust*, 113.

Holocaust (pages 38–43)

1. Kershaw, *Hitler, 1936–1945: Nemesis*, 153.

2. *Ibid.*, 171.

3. *Ibid.*, 145.

4. Gilbert, *The Holocaust*, 82.

5. *Ibid.*, 99.

6. US Holocaust Memorial Museum, "Introduction to the Holocaust", http://www.ushmm.org/wlc/en/article.php?ModuleId=10005143.

7. US Holocaust Memorial Museum, "Ghettoes", http://www.ushmm.org/wlc/en/article.php?ModuleId=10005059.

8. Gilbert, *The Holocaust*, 127.

9. *Ibid.*, 176.

10. *Ibid.*, 219–21.

11. Fischer, *The History of an Obsession*, 350.

12. Longerich, *Holocaust*, 306.

13. Fischer, *The History of an Obsession*, 295–97.

14. Longerich, *Holocaust*, 309.

15. Fischer, *The History of an Obsession*, 357.

16. *Ibid.*, 357.

17. US Holocaust Memorial Museum, "The Holocaust and World War II: Timeline", http://www.ushmm.org/wlc/en/article.php?ModuleId=10007653.

Hitler's legacy (pages 44–49)

1. Stephanie Fitzgerald, *Children of the Holocaust* (Oxford: Capstone Press, 2011), 4.

2. *Haaretz*, "Israel Closes Decade with Population of 7.5 Million", 30 December 2009, http://www.haaretz.com/news/israel-closes-decade-with-population-of-7-5-million-1.1083; and US Census Bureau, "Total Ancestry Reported", http://factfinder2.census.gov/faces/tableservices/jsf/pages/productview.xhtml?pid=ACS_10_1YR_B04003&prodType=table.

3. Yad Vashem, "The Holocaust Resource Center: Frequently Asked Questions", http://www1.yadvashem.org/yv/en/holocaust/resource_center/faq.asp.

4. Second World War History, "World War 2 Casualty Statistics", http://www.secondworldwarhistory.com/world-war-2-statistics.asp.

5. Kershaw, *Hitler, 1936–1945: Nemesis*, 840.

6. Fischer, *The History of an Obsession*, 405.

7. Kershaw, *Hitler, 1936–1945: Nemesis*, 838.

8. Fischer, *The History of an Obsession*, 361.

9. *Ibid.*, 362.

10. Simon Wiesenthal Centre, "Adolf Eichmann", http://www.ushmm.org/wlc/en/article.php?ModuleId=10007412.

11. Kershaw, *Hitler, 1936–1945: Nemesis*, 841.

12. US Holocaust Memorial Museum, "Holocaust Denial Timeline", http://www.ushmm.org/wlc/en/article.php?ModuleId=10008003.

13. *Ibid.*

What if? (pages 50–51)

1. Fischer, *The History of an Obsession*, 399.

The road to genocide (pages 52–53)

1. Kershaw, *Hitler, 1936–1945: Nemesis*, 155.

Glossary

Allied belonging to the Allies (see below)

Allies group of nations opposed to Germany and other countries during World War II; major Allies include Britain, France, the Soviet Union, and the United States

anti-Semite someone who hates Jewish people

anti-Semitism hatred of Jews

Arab member of the Arabic-speaking people, many of whom live in the Arabian countries of the Middle East

Aryan term used by the Nazis to describe a non-Jewish Caucasian, supposedly part of a master race

atrocity act of extreme cruelty or savage violence

Bolshevik relating to the revolutionary socialist movement that took power in Russia in 1917

boycott refuse to take part in or deal with

capitalist member of an economic system in which the means of making and moving products are owned by private people and companies rather than by the government

chancellor (in Germany) the head of the government

civilian person who is not in the armed forces

communist relating to the social and political system in which property and the means of production are owned by the people of the country

concentration camp camp where political prisoners, prisoners of war, and refugees are imprisoned together

death camp camp where people are brought so that they can be systematically killed

depression in economics, a time of drastic decline in an economy, with falling trade, prices, and employment

dictator ruler who has complete control over a nation and its people

discrimination treating a person differently because of something such as his or her race or gender

emigrant someone who moves out of or away from their country

emigrate move out of or away from a country

emigration movement of people from one country to another

extermination getting rid of something by destroying it completely

extremist person who uses or campaigns for extreme measures to get what he or she wants (especially in politics or religion)

fascism system of government in which control is in the hands of extreme right-wing and nationalist rulers

führer German word for "leader"

genocide planned destruction of a racial, religious, ethnic, national, or political group of people

Gestapo secret police organization founded by the Nazis; the word is short for the German *Geheime Staatspolizei* (Secret State Police)

ghetto in World War II, section of a city where Jews or other minority groups were confined

holocaust widespread or horrific destruction. "The Holocaust" now refers specifically to the mass murder of Jews by the Nazis. In its original sense, holocaust means burnt offering, which is why some people prefer the term Shoah, meaning catastrophe, to describe the tragedy.

industrialist someone who owns or manages a large business involved with manufacturing or trade

legacy something which is left by somebody for future generations

liberate free or release from something

loot to steal something by force

massacre to kill a large number of people

nationalist person who fights for the unity or interests of a single nation

Nazi member of the German National Socialist Worker's Party, led by Hitler from 1921

persecute to harass or harm someone because of their nationality, or their political or religious views

persecution act of harassing someone because of their nationality or beliefs

pogrom organized massacre of a people, such as Jews

propaganda spreading of true or false information in order to bring about change, or to promote a belief or movement

putsch sudden rebellion or attempt to seize power

racist someone who discriminates against another person because of their racial origins

rearmament obtaining or manufacturing of a new stock of weapons

refugee person forced to flee his or her home due to war or natural disaster

Reichstag German parliament and parliament building in Berlin

Roma travelling people who speak the Romany language; they are also known as "gypsies"

SA (short for "*Sturmabteilung*," or "Storm Section") private army formed by Hitler in 1921 to intimidate his rivals and to protect him from attacks; also known as storm troopers

sanction penalty measure taken by a country or group of countries against another that has violated international laws

Soviet Union nation, formerly Russia, that controlled much of Eastern Europe from 1922 to 1991

SS (short for "*Schutzstaffel*", or "Protection Squadron") paramilitary security force founded by the Nazis, which was used for many brutal jobs, including running death camps and murdering possible opponents

storm trooper member of the SA

synagogue Jewish place of worship

find out more

World War II ended nearly 70 years ago. Since then, a vast amount of evidence, eyewitness accounts, statistics, and historical analysis has been published. So, there is no shortage of raw material for research through books, films, and the internet. Here is just a small selection of useful sources.

Books

Adolf Hitler (Famous Lives), Katie Daynes (Usborne, 2006)

The Diary of a Young Girl, Anne Frank (Alfred A. Knopf, 2010)

The Holocaust (Documenting World War II), Neil Tong (Wayland, 2012)

The Rise of the Nazis (Documenting World War II), Neil Tong (Wayland, 2012)

World War II (Dorling Kindersley, 2012)

DVDs

Documentaries
Into the Arms of Strangers (Warner Home Video, 2000)
This documentary is about the *kindertransports* – the evacuation of Jewish children from Germany to Britain.

The World at War (1973; New Video, 2004)
This classic television documentary has 26 parts.

World War II (A&E/New Video, 2009)
This 10-disc set covers the conflict's full history, with interviews and archive footage.

Fiction
Life Is Beautiful (1999; Buena Vista Home Video, 2000)
This haunting film finds comedy in the face of the tragedy of the Jewish deportations.

Websites

Caution: These sites may contain material that is upsetting or disturbing.

www.bbc.co.uk/history/people/adolf_hitler
Learn more about Hitler and the events of World War II on the BBC website.

www.holocaust-history.org
This is one of the best general sites about the Holocaust.

www.iwm.org.uk
The Imperial War Museum website has lots of information about World War II, including photographic collections of Hitler. If you live in London, you could even pay the museum a visit.

www.yadvashem.org
Yad Vashem is the research centre and living memorial to the Holocaust produced by the Jewish people.

Other topics to research

- Fascism in other parts of Europe in the 1930s (especially Italy and Spain).

- How remarkable Jewish refugees (such as Einstein) influenced their new homelands.

- How modern Israel was founded and developed.

- Coming to terms with shame: the post-war journey of Germany.

- The work of Simon Wiesenthal and other post-war Nazi hunters.

Index